HATHOR'S
Love Lessons

VOLUME I

HATHOR

Copyright © 2024 Hathor.

All rights reserved. No part of this book may be reproduced, stored, or transmitted by any means—whether auditory, graphic, mechanical, or electronic—without written permission of both publisher and author, except in the case of brief excerpts used in critical articles and reviews. Unauthorized reproduction of any part of this work is illegal and is punishable by law.

ISBN: 978-1-63950-282-0 (sc)
ISBN: 978-1-63950-284-4 (hc)
ISBN: 978-1-63950-285-1 (e)

This publication contains the opinions and ideas of its author. It is intended to provide helpful and informative material on the subjects addressed in the publication. The author and publisher specifically disclaim all responsibility for any liability, loss, or risk, personal or otherwise, which is incurred as a consequence, directly or indirectly, of the use and application of any of the contents of this book.

Gateway Towards Success

8063 MADISON AVE #1252
Indianapolis, IN 46227
+13176596889
www.writersapex.com

Contents

Introduction 1
Dedication 3
Love 4
Grand Union 5
Purpose 6
Divinity 7
My Path… 8
I Surrender 9
No Regret 11
Empathy 14
Change 18
New Vision 23
A Woman's Love 24
Jewels Of Mine 26
Reflections 27
Intuition 29
Matriarchal Insight 30
Silent Wars of Love 32
Self Discipline 34
Hear Me 35
Confessions of a Soul in Search of… 36
Your Judgement Does Not Matter 39
Learn From Mistakes 40
Under the Spell 41
Accepting His Mind Over Mind 43

We Can Talk About It 44
I Forget About Me Loving You Sometimes 45
I Am A Wombman 47
Freedom 48
Blessing In Disguise 49
Pray For Them 50
Ungrateful 51
Soul Purpose 52
I Am Not A Victim 53
To Just Simply Be 54
All I Have 55
Fake Friends 56
Checking On Me 57
Abuse 58
Street Shit 59
No Hate 61
No Hate Pt2 62
We Live On The Air 63
Inner Peace 64

Introduction

Greetings!

Welcome to Hathors Temple Of Love Vol 1.

Within these sacred pages of the divine womb holder, you shall gain eternal wisdom.

As you embark on this divine path, I request you open your heart seat. Allow these poems to relate, heal, and release while expressing transforming energy. Discovering myself has revealed my ability to become still. Within stillness, I'm harnessing the virtues of patience and self-love. Learning how to ask, surrender, and receive from this mystical power that gives us life. This power translates as the ability to create life's expressions effortlessly. The heart center is the seat of creation and expression. It is what transcends our thoughts, and feelings into reality.

This is much more than a poetry book expressing notions of love. The wise will realize the jewels within this book. By the various wisdom gained throughout the years of self-discovery, my awareness, and consciousness have guided me to turn these elements into earthly jewels. I am continuously unlearning, learning, and expanding my consciousness while practicing the art of stillness and patience.

The greatest expression of my being is the compassion I've developed for myself and humanity. Sharing these love lessons is a gift I humbly present to you. We are all connected by this great human experience related to our emotions. These poems are my expression of my True soul. As you read I hope you can reflect on your own experiences in this life. May these poems awaken the many stages of growth and change in you as it's done for me. I am grateful for the ability to express what's within me.

Serving Humanity while living out my design by natural nature.

As'e

Hathor Godesss Of Love...

Dedication

First off I would like to thank the people in my life who have supported me by encouraging my self-expression and creativity. I would also like to thank those who attempted to silence and suppress my voice. It was a perfect balance teaching me lessons to strengthen my mind and empower my growth in becoming this soul I am. I realize all the experiences I have encountered in life was for my story, my truth along this journey. I am grateful for knowing this sacred wisdom. I dedicate these poems/psalms to my ancestors. Matriarchal klan mothers aka Sybils also Patriarchal Czars, healers prophets, and prophetess. Thank you for blessing me with the Power of words and the gift of prophecies. I am greatly grateful for your guidance, strength, protection, and love. I could not have started or completed this project without it.

Let me reintroduce you to poetry in motion, the art of spoken words. To my beautiful children whom I so dearly love and respect for your unique personalities, thank you for teaching me every day a little bit more about myself by Seeing life through your eyes. My prayer is for your lives to be filled with happiness and joy. I love you all forever, thank you for the encouragement and motivation.

Dedicated to: *MAMI* and the *GREAT SYBILS*

When you speak… you speak for many

We speak through you

The mission is truth

Love

Love what do you have in store for me
I embrace love with open arms
the lessons you have to teach me
The secrets within my heart
Love you lead me and I shall follow
Eager yet patient and ever ready for all the omniverse has to give
I shall receive abundantly
My cup shall be filled forever in the kingdom of divine love
May my ancestors grant me guidance
protection
wisdom
intuition
May all my questions be answered
May I learn stillness
In stillness
Life reveals
Revelations of the unknown
I am thankful
I am greatful
I bless myself with my energy
I heal myself with my energy
I love myself with my energy
I alter everyone I come into contact with my energy
For the greatest good
remember who you are
now say
I am Powerful
I AM

Grand Union

I thank the ancestors for bringing us together
In this union of friendship and love
I thank the ancestors for opening my heart
I'm thankful for the joy and blessings
Thankful for the ability to love someone besides myself
Are you my twin flame
I call you my soul mate
I think we are tied together in a harmonious love
Involving all the elements from creation working as one
We fight for the freedom of our people to become liberated
To sustain life on this earth
we love
we hurt
we heal
we love
we grow
we evolve
I see a reflection of similar qualities
What is it like to truly be free
Taking off the mask of who I use to be
Revealing the essence of me

Purpose

Life is purposeful
We often ask what is our purpose
That is a journey within, one must find by
going, within and becoming still
As long as your alive you have a purpose
When you fulfill a purpose another presents itself
One keeps on fulfilling purposes until they reach
their ultimate divine purpose/potential
How do you know
By all the souls you've touched and helped along the way
The impact you have on others
It's a path and training grounds leading to your journey
All you have to do is place yourself within

space

time

mind

Allow the divine to mold you into all you shall become
The work is already done
The blueprint of your being is encoded in your genetics
Life experiences will activate it

Divinity

Is your soul satisfied

have you lived the visions you visualize in the mind

What are you waiting for

Laying down a brick one day at a time

A foundation that represents my integrity

I have to live with the essence of me

I have to dig deeper to find peace

Staying in the flow

I thought you loved me it isn't so

What you say and how I feel confuse the mind

However I shall continue to rise

Truth speaks clear and with intent

To lift one up and give direction

With a purpose to persevere

I am no victim

I am a creator

I am a character molder

I am a innovator

I have to decide now or later

Im being show the signs

I will not hold on to what

Serves me no more in my life

My Path...

The path I'm on is Divine
The mission is to free the mind
Our works are spiritual
Rising with the sun
Flowing with the tides
I grow stronger and stronger
There are no obstacles
Only emotions that surface inside
It can cause confusion
Become still
My soul speaks
Let it flow through you,
something is affecting you
Awareness
Your job is to figure it out
It feels like a death in the Depths of my womb
it is a wound
where did it come from
This energy creeping in so deadly
Tormenting it can be
changing the chemistry of my mind
I'm fighting internally to survive
The question I ask myself is why
I demand the god in me to awake
Give me the power to
Change this fate
this is not who I want to be
A prisoner of hurt
trauma set free

I Surrender

I surrender these tears

I surrender my life

I surrender these years

Of wandering with no direction or purpose

Not knowing who I am

A lost soul

Allowing myself to be manipulated

I am anointed

I am Godchild

I surrender for a higher awakening to innerstand

I surrender for truth

I surrender to the divine within me for healing

No longer will I fight against what I'm given

lessons in the form of blessings

Proceeding with life

I will not allow anyone or thing outside me to dim my light

I can obtain peace it's all in my mind

I am greatful

I have no regrets when I was loving you

Apart of me still do

I sacrificed because I wanted to

Yet now I must do what I need to do

So the god in me can see

So the god in me can be

No suppression

No control only over my emotions

So I can reflect true soul

If I had to do it all over again I would

No regrets

Learning to love myself the way I should

Spiritual growth is the most painful

Yet I emerge out this cocoon so beautiful

so beautiful

Like a butterfly, I spread my wings and fly

You had my heart for that season

Now it's time I arrived

I feel so alive inside

I have no regrets

no regrets

I realize it was just an experience

No need to hold onto unhealthy emotions or memories

I'll remember the good times

I'll think of you and smile

Love is continuous

yet this is the part where the pain ends

No Regret

All that was broken will surely mend

I wish you well

no regrets

I wish you well

I have no regrets

cause I accept

All we experienced were tests

I have no regrets

I have no regrets

I have no regrets

Thankful for my blessing

Truth I accept

My path I accept

My path I accept

My life will be filled with spiritual wealth

I have to let go

Just know I loved you so

I have no regrets

Maybe we may love again

Yet now I have to walk again

I have to go

The winds of uncertainty who knows

I loved you with all my soul

No regrets

I'll love you until my last breath

No regrets
We created life
No regrets
I survived death
No regrets
Energy and time given
No regrets
I had to reshape my mind
No regrets
All the tears I cried
No regrets
The pain from our fights
No regret
We hurt each other with words
No regret
Greatful for the lessons learned
No regret
I sacrificed it all, no regrets
It made me strong, no regrets
Preparing me for the next chapter
I have a better overstanding of myself
It's a freedom that comes with love
Liberation
Never binding
Unconditional

No judgement

Unbreakable trust

Truth inspires growth

uncomfortable at times

where am I going

The path is unknown

The past seems so familiar

Yet if I hold on to the vision of the future

I will make it

I will make it through the storms of my heart

I will make it through the doubts of my mind

I will make it through the uneasy feelings that reside

I will make it through the night

within me shines a light

so bright

A vision is all I have

A vision of who I am

Empathy

This path feels lonely

We started off with love

Does anyone understand

I wish I had company

Yet it's not part of the divines plan

So much wisdom I've gained

So much more to learn

So much more growth is ahead of me

Doors waiting to open

What is to become of me

I walked away from the familiar

It hurts real bad

Betrayal

It hurts real bad

When intentions are not real

laugh at my hurt

I speak life into my dreams

bask at my falls

My mysery brings them joy

look at me

How can you be my friend

what is love

I need to love myself again

I was on a hospital table fighting for my life

My daughter was born

love you left me with no care

what is life

what is death

That is a hard pill to swallow

The truth

is it a competition

to see who's hurt is worse

I have to remove myself from this hell

I have to undo this spell

A new cipher

those who care

Who will celebrate my happiness

With them I can share

what is a friend

I've learned to be a friend to myself

I realized what I seek on the outside

I need to become

It's a awakening for me

Closing the chapter to some

I give

I give

I give

and end up with none

This equation isn't equal

Truest sum is one

My energy was utilized by others

that's what I call life using you

When you don't know your purpose

You have no voice of truth

So no matter how it hurts to understand

I am greatful for this day

Today I take a stand

I let go of my past

I let go of my pain

I let go of the anger that came with mistreatments and rage

For the awakening of my soul

I was asleep

I did all I could to hinder sight

in disbelief

Those I once called family

were dealing in deceit

shattered my reality and I became weak

Became sick because of a broken heart

It took some time to heal and adjust my mind

I didn't realize this power within
so once again
I rise from my fall
starting over
A new beginning
I must have fell a thousand times
I must have cried so much
I bruised my insides
Spirit is fighting to live
I must fulfill what I came to give
no matter how challenging
I will not give up on myself

Change

These words spoken

were they meant to be spells cast on me

I open my mind

I opened my heart

I opened my being to you

It's starting a war within

trying to replace my truth with yours

It confuses me

Mental manipulation

Your using me

I'm no victim

Just need air to speak

I let you in my head

For many nights I couldn't sleep

A bright future ahead

I could not see

Your vision is not mine

It's blinding me

I am in darkness right now

Overwhelmed by the light

You reversed everything in my mind

something isn't right

I have to make sense of this

I must overcome

This is mental

This is detrimental

Is this love

Fighting for my life to redeem my soul

I gave you power to torment me so I can feel whole

So I was incomplete from the beginning

Wounded soul

Searching amid misery

I realized this was not the way

So deeply rooted how can I make a way

How can I change

Hathors Love Lessons

Lesson 1

Never love a man more than you love yourself

Lesson 2

Never place ANYONE before your children

He will abuse his power when you don't bend to his every whim

He will take you on a ride that is unforgettable

With your permission of course

So your not the victim

It's never his fault

You will be broken down and used

Your fears will be pacified

Your mind confused and abused

That's the art of master manipulation

It's never his fault always yours
He replaces your mind with his views
The brainwashing begins
The reasoning behind all that's happening
you opened your temple
your vortex to this
It all started with a conversation
A kiss
He will use your weakness to build his strength
He will use your energy and time to build his wealth
You will become a convenience because he has learned you
You're a liar in all you say
A slanderer in all you do
sitting with bowed head
staring with ready eyes
An unimaginable pain
No one can hear your cries
He will rationalize
Learning you is an art
he has mastered
you begin to fall into a deep black hole of emptiness
Praying to wake from this nightmare
Body mind soul indicates this ain't what you need
Will you ever find the strength to leave
He will guilt you into staying
Why stay and pay the price for a heart you didn't break
why stay in this emotional turmoil

Don't give no one power over your soul
They will bring you down so low
Feels as if you are living in two worlds
Everyone becomes a liar or hateful
Who cares for you
This is his bird eye view
So they can't reach you
Swimming in a sea of darkness
Looking for a life saver
To save her
How do I save her
She's getting use to this treatment
Verbal abuse
emotionally empty
spiritually empty
Soul feels neglected you see
How low I was brought down
I was not made to die
I was created to fly
Once you cry and cry and cry
Keep making excuses
Stubborn love
To try and try and try
universal truth you can't deny
One day those tears will dry
You will command change in your life and rise

You have to want it

You have to embrace it

You have to taste it

You have to visualize it

To receive it

Accept it

Don't fear it

Breathe it

Believe it

You shall rise out of this

You start by making different choices

The only one who can do this is you

The only one who can win this battle is you

Make up your mind to rise

Embrace nature's help in your life

All you have to do is make up your mind

And all things will align

Tunnel vision

Focus your mind

All things take time

New Vision

Today I wake up and realize

Life is a gift

I get to see life through different eyes

My own..

Feel the warmth of the sunshine

I give thanks for this simple gift

The way it warms my skin

I am in bliss

I'm greatful to be able to enjoy this

I am greatful to see my life's worth

For a long time I thought love I didn't deserve

I thought happiness was something earned

That I had to give others to receive

Yet I've learned

Walk a path of truth

Discern All that hinders your growth

I look at the trees as the wind blows with ease

moving their leaves

I feel the gentleness of the breeze

Shouldn't life be enjoyable I think to myself

By my thoughts I'm pleased

A Woman's Love

When a woman loves
She gives her all
A woman may go against what seems right to love
When a woman loves
She takes you into her soul
It becomes your home
she cooks and cleans
nurture and support all you do
She loves and cares
whatever is hers becomes yours to share
When a woman loves
she gives her all
She forgives a unknowing past
She ignores the rumors from those wishing this love won't last
When a woman loves
She loves hard
Down to the last sweet drop
It's the greatest symphony of old-school rhythm and blues
Summer Sunday jazz blowing melodic horns
Excites the senses with goosebumps from harmonic notes
Stirring memories of a foreign past
loving a man like you makes me feel whole

Your strong

Patient

Hard-working

disciplined

Loving to

Strumming the strings of my heart-shaped guitar

This is what you do

Hazy summer days and cool summer night

We dance a grand dance of life

Quenching each other's thirst like a cool glass of lemonade

At first, I didn't understand you

I paid a price getting to know you

you captivated my heart

You mesmerized my mind

Your charismatic nature has pulled my deep waters inside

We fought wars

We traveled many moons

We sacrificed it all

Reason we have it all

We gave that which we seek

Jewels Of Mine

My fruits have grown

From the seeds I've planted

My fruits have grown

From the environment, it survived

My fruits have grown

from the many lessons I've taught

Creations of my mind

I sit back and listen as they teach me

Look how time, has advanced their mind

Experiences shaped their reality

Self speaks truth and they decide

They acknowledge my struggles

Stare apon my Bare naked insides

Youthful eyes

Untainted they look on

Fearless they look on

They look at my scars

However judgeless

Attentive to every word being spoken

Alertness

Reflections

As I stare upon this rose

It's essence

Its love

petals unfold

The layers reveal their secrets

Bitter sweet aroma

joys and pains

Tears from departures

Laughter with loving intent

Leaving not one cell untouched

From its energy

From its strength

To get up and fly again

The phoenix rises from her ashes

Twisted tides with notions of paradise

Lessons unfolding before my eyes

Venom from kisses blinding sight

Fighting for the same cause

Are we fighting on the same sides

Why do I feel conflicted inside

Listening to our hearts
Listen to our minds
Guidance through the wind chimes
Melodies activating keys F-A-C
Elevating my higher chi
Ascending from the chains of a conditioned broken heart
Awareness of what I allow into my temple
training my mind to resist stress
Convinced myself to fall asleep
The numbness deflects my conscience
Yet silence was still loud
And feelings were still triggered by your responses
Your words induced me into spells of enchantment
Where truth was far away from me
My fantasy became my reality
My reality became the outward cry of me

Intuition

Complacent with my hurt

I distantly pushed it aside

Empathetic towards your thoughts and wounded pride

Disciplining my ego and internal cries

Perhaps looking for approval in your eyes

All I needed from you was a smile

All I needed were a few kind words

All I needed was a phone call

Is this an overdose on love?

Am I going through withdrawal?

Why do you have this affect on me..?

Creating where there were no insecurities

Twisting my truths

Replacing the living word with you

Ancestral tidal waves are roaring in my solar plexus

An invader is present

Trauma

Traumatic childhood

Nervousness

Anxiety

Scared

I thank you for revealing what was hidden

Matriarchal Insight

I am as gentle as a morning breeze

Rest your thoughts

Set your mind at ease

As I pull you into

my waters

fulfilling all your needs

Warm as the sun

Shining onto these leaves

Who am I

They call me the golden one

She who pleases

Many names know me

My roots are strong and deeply grounded in the earth

I am soft and delicate like rose petals

Sweet as the aroma of flowers

Natural Nature grew me for all to see

As I shall be the anticipation rising subtlety

For this purpose, nature groomed me to be

You are invited to see my works

Like the lotus my flower blooms

I am a sun often mistaken for a moon

I am MAMI

My suns, I created har

Hat Har distant house from a far

Denderah that glitch beyond the stars

Who am I

Let me reintroduce you

By my powers of attraction, I shall seduce you

Brain concentration became an attraction

Pleasures, rhythmic movement, and graceful actions

I am true womanhood

I live beyond the stars and exist with time

Who am I

I exist in the creation of mind

It is I

You call upon when performing prayer and libations

My eyes command you to realize

My smile mesmerizes

Matriarch rise

It is time for us to take our place

Justly rule with order and grace

Natural nature shall take its course

Life flows through MAMI pores

Silent Wars of Love

He deals with subtle control
His silence speaks loud
Abuse is his absence
Yet and still I wear my crown
I'm striving to become better, learning myself
Not seeking his approval, only the true love for myself
Freedom to express my creativity
Yet I obey and love him intently
I can't have both
satisfying him hinders me
Our Love turns into a competition
Ego and tribal wars
Which one of us will win
These are the silent wars of love
Waters stirring deep in my womb
Warm and cold tides collide
Yet peace exists in the midst of all this
My mind is at peace
I don't judge him, I accept him
I embrace him, I relate to him
I allow his words to mold me because he is so great
Even in the moment of our hearts racing
I must still my mind, I must find my voice

I shall, I will be triumphant

Stubbornly I will love him

Despite all the red flags and signs

Pridefully I will love him

Past the warnings and his drama-filled life

The audacity of me, praying it will manifest in time

This is how it begins

defiling and lying to self

As God silently watches

A great sin

Temptation

Self Discipline

I don't want to be bitter

Nor do I want to have an attitude

You know I'll do whatever it takes to put you in the mood

Can you give me the affection I need

Say you'll love me endlessly

Commit to me

Is love easy

I'm willing to give my all at your request

I must be strong not to lose myself

Loving someone like you is challenging

I must discipline myself in the art of loving you

Hear Me

The same way men are able to deal with the sexual side of a woman

They should be prepared to innerstand our emotions

Emotions are connected to the womb

The breath of life

E-motions linked to mental-mind

Thoughts and feelings

A woman's emotions are fragile

For a woman who is intuned, emotions are intuitive

Confessions of a Soul in Search of...

I feel sad right now

I'm not certain if this is the correct emotion I should feel

Yet tears are flowing from my eyes

I have a stiffness in my throat

How can anyone have such power over me

I allowed it because of the love I feel for you

Now I'm realizing this may be the price to pay

How does one deal with such narcissistic behavior displayed

I chose not to respond or react

Quieting the empath within and becoming numb

How did we get here

By choosing to see good in an abused, hurt, tormented soul

Attempts to weaken me

my light is still lit seeing good in all things, even this

Insensitive to my feelings

He does not care about my needs

These are my feelings

Emotional intelligence, focusing on my higher self

Questioning my emotions and mind

I can exist in this relationship detached

Now you are showing your true colors

It's killing the attraction I felt towards you

It is my punishment for pursuing my dreams

Emotional manipulation

A mental tactic noted

Making alot of money, independent, I sense jealousy
He wants to control me, so this is the mind game he plays
Using a child to manipulate
I'm the secretary, he has a child doing the things he asked me to do
My punishment for not sticking up under
him the way he wants me to
Subliminal message you can be replaced by someone
inadequate and not equivalent to you.
Using the lower to throw off higher frequencies
maim all attempts of happiness to rule my energy
I want to talk to him yet I choose silence
He's conditioned to be rational with aggression and rage
purposely done to silence me
communication is breached
I see through his facade
This is his grooming of me
Why am I here?
Wasting my time
Tactics staged to bring me into a slave submission
in disguise as a need for help
what is my purpose here
Is this the role of his wife?
MY STRENGTH takes over the weakness
of being blinded by my sight
I AM THE GODDESS OF LOVE!

This is my domain and I rule!
I will not be broken down by the likes of you!
I will stay in grace of who I am!
Matriarchal blood flows through me you better learn and understand!
I shall not run from any obstacle I will overcome!
With divinity in my wings the chosen one!
You forget I am HATHOR
You pursued me
Don't get comfortable because of the passion
and love I fed to your needs
I made you feel invincible, I made you feel strong
Yet I can also break you down with my absence
and make you feel very small
When I choose to walk away your world will fall apart
Because you did not love me equally with a pure heart
The most desired, beautiful and wanted she chose you
Had those who hate you take a second look to see what I saw in you
Some men who possess diamonds are damn fools
When I leave all your blessing will also
Stripped from titles ranks position will follow
Great ancestors flow through the blood in these veins
You shall not destroy me
This is your KARMA MAMI grants you for all your wrong

Your Judgement Does Not Matter

I'm doing what I was chosen to do
I will fulfill my purpose with no regards
of how you choose to judge me
What are judgements but perceptions of how one thinks
Are they true or limited by a person's mental IQ?

Learn From Mistakes

I will continue to love
Make mistakes, learn from them
Be happy
Obtain inner peace
Strive for a still mind
Be kind and loving to others
Be kind to myself
Relax and take it easy
One day at a time

Under the Spell

I am grateful I no longer work at the hair salon
Although one of my goals is to own my shop one day
Check game...
I was told by the man I love, that I don't need to
touch others in this growth period of my life
I thought his care was sincere.
However, All it was, was control
My energy needs to be harnessed, it's sacred and it isn't for everyone
I was so thankful to accept his guidance as a sign from the universe
How naive I once seemed, so innocent and trustworthy
I hugged his words as if my creator spoke them
I listened to him because I trusted him
I shared my goals and dreams with him because I trusted him
He was only attempting to slow me down and keep me off my path
Fear I would become greater than him
Fear I would awake from sleep
Jealous of my Freedom to choose how I live my life
I'm not stuck or stagnated like him
Caught in a lie glitch effect
A cult way of living

Religion can uplift and inspire the greatest potential in human beings
Religion can also be used to control the minds of the vulnerable
control the minds of those lost and seeking
control the minds of the hurt and hungry
control the minds of the abused and traumatized
The spell is real
Sisters and brothers wake up
Be careful
deal with everyone who comes onto your path
with a steady hand and watchful eye
yes, I knew yet when we open our hearts and let our
guard down we become vulnerable and weak
unless you know you really won't know
it's all chance however please protect what's sacred to you
be it your heart, your soul, your mind, your children, your dreams

Accepting His Mind Over Mind

His silence makes me think
His silence reveals my joys and fears
His silence shows me truth
His silence replaces the physical abuse
His silence shows his disapproval
His silence reflects his love
So many thoughts surface
Yet I am reminded by my higher self to stay positive
By his words, I am comforted and reminded not to cast any judgment
Love is patient
Love is kind
Love is compassion
Love is understanding
Glimpses of memories where his kindness made me feel safe
Has me seeking that feeling from him once again
His smile mesmerizing
His love attainable
The effect he has on my soul makes me love him even more
I am anticipating getting past his silence
and continuing where we left off
By his silence I am reminded not to react,
it is my choice to respond or not
Has me thinking I must live out the
expression of my equation lovingly
All I can do is be who I was created to be
I show my love, my support, my compassion
Even in the midst of his silence he still controls me
His silence is very loud

We Can Talk About It

We can talk about it, love

We can talk about it, love

We can talk about it, let's start living it

We can talk about it till the sun sets

We can talk about it till the moon rise

All we do is talk about it

Let's start applying to live a beautiful life

If you ask me the cost

I'm willing to sacrifice my feelings

Just for this love I'll grow up and change my dealing's

Molding my mind to be one of a kind

To match your maturity because you're the one I love

I'm willing to learn

I'm willing to grow

I'm willing to put in work

Not afraid to cry

Not afraid to try

let's deal with the truth

no lies

If that's what it takes for us to survive

I Forget About Me Loving You Sometimes

Walking in between social lines and roles

Ego is a social mask some wear

Loving you is easy

I understand your Nature

I'm sweet yet strong

bittersweet love

You take advantage of my kindness

I can support you

by being your backbone

In the process forget about me

What makes me happy

What makes me smile

Get so caught up loving you, I forget me sometimes

I have to walk in between the lines, yes I do

It's all about balancement, this is my truth from loving you

I accept the lesson which is a gift

You teach indirectly, I like to thank you for this experience

Learning how to love you and myself to

Ill jump at the drop of a dime, just to make you happy

Ill invest all my time because you want it baby

However, I've noticed when your wrapped up in you

The way you treat me, how you do

I question your heart

At times you talk to me as if my feelings are not there
It only makes me stronger
Is this the survivor or ego not wanting to be wrong about you
No one told me love would be this way
I am uncritical because I want you to stay
I want peace and understanding between you and I
Let's build a tribe
I'm by your side
I'm not going to force, pull or try to change anything
I accept the seasons and all the blessings they bring
I respect you, king
Giving unconditional love

I Am A Wombman

Yes I am A wombman

Don't mean I need you any less because I'm strong

Strength is not a badge of honor I wear

Its hidden and revealed when its presence is needed

Yet I can not change what you see in me

Nor will I deny what I inherited from my great ancestral bloodline

Don't take advantage of me or play me for a fool

I revealed my vulnerability to you

I've shown you I'm soft

Yes I'm a woman

I'm Tender to the touch

Delicate...

Beautiful...

Natural...

Freedom

My mind is not indoctrinated nor confounded by a belief system

I am a spiritual being

You will not get me to commit sins against my ancestors

Stand for what they were against

Betray a bloodline that forbid ignorance

Blessing In Disguise

You are amazing, sweet destiny

You are my serenity

You are my truth

I'm so grateful for you

How can something so pure be created from what was unsure

All the things I've endured

You are my cure

Pray For Them

I pray for them

They cannot see

I pray for them

They don't feel

I pray for them

They don't know

I pray for them

They are stagnated with no growth

I pray for them

They hurt themselves

I pray for them

They care for no one but their selves

I pray for them

Who knew of the lie

I pray for them instead of despise

I pray for them

I can feel their guilt

Look at their lives incomplete

Seeking the innocent and youth

To carry on the conspiracy of covering the truth

Ungrateful

You never said thank you for all the things I've done for you

You never appreciated me

I sacrificed my time and energy

I gave of myself

While your eyes disguised the lies

Their lurked a sneakiness behind your smile

My energy goes off vibes

Conflicting with my mind

Intuition warning me things are not right

My ancestors watched on patiently

Awaiting the moment to awaken me

I cooked

I cleaned

I worked

I was a slave for you

Catering to your every need

I gave and you took selfishly

Karma eventually turned the tables around

Now you're the one drowning in your deeds

I still showed you love because I believe

You never kick anyone when their down

Despite your attempts to trample me to the ground

I loved more than my ability

provided a mother's love and patience you never received

Unconditional love you cannot grasp nor perceive

Soul Purpose

If the souls purpose is to connect to where it came from
If the souls purpose is to link back to simplistic rites
Then the voices of the ancestors will surely
guide those who have lost their sight
Yet even those who choose to stay blind
If the blood link to completion is strong and divine
Ancestors will fight and guide
My prayer is to give sight to the blind
Quiet the mentally insane mind
Bring comfort to those in pain
This request I ask in the ancestor's name

I Am Not A Victim

I will not allow myself to become a victim

I will not allow myself to become broken

I will allow strength and healing to replace my pain

I will reflect on the lessons learned

Reclaim my throne

Equipt my mental

Enhance my soul

Never regretful

Forever Grateful

My worth is much more than gold

I am priceless

For I serve a higher purpose

Divine Potentiality

To Just Simply Be

I will not allow my ship to sink

I will not allow my pain to conquer me

Outside there are no answers for truth resides in me

I allow myself to be

I allow myself to heal

I allow myself to deal and face all that is in front of me

All I Have

If all I have are my thoughts and words to comfort me then so be it
My chest is heavy and my throat feels clogged
could it be despair
My breath can barely ease the stress or pain
my body feels from heartbreak
It feels like I was in a boxing match and took so
much body shots that I'm losing strength
My mind is telling me stay on your feet yet
physically and emotionally I feel weak
I don't want to carry any resentment or anger
Lessons in understanding my hurt and
forgiveness flows freely through me
Having empathy for my torturer, who uses
the tool of silence to attack me
Which for now in my eyes is the enemy of my
self-expression and communication
There is a disconnection
I will not take part in this relation
I will not accept this

Fake Friends

Fake friends
Fake sisters
Fake brothers
How can you tell
They only call or remember you, when they are in need
Users take advantage of those who display good deeds
Good hearts, why
Self speaks, unlike them you are dependable
Your word is your bond
You appreciate and cherish it as life
You care and they don't
Self speaks, the air you breathe smites cruel intentions
Energy unveils deceit and disguises
A disease, jealousy lingers
You are what they are not

Checking On Me

My heart is going through many changes
Or shall I say
The poison is slowly coming out
Raindrops fall from my eyes
Yet and still I smile
I am alive, I survived
I now know what it means to love myself unconditionally

Abuse

Before getting to know one
A conscious mind is awake at all times
If not awake or aware
Here is a reminder
Abuser- one who is out of control with self
Yet demands others to be under control
Using mental manipulation
Emotional manipulation and unnecessary force

Street Shit

Niggaz be on sum turn you down, dumb down shit
I elevate my mind
Exist in pure bliss
Heaven is this
Yet respectful minds are hard to find
Constant game
To be around dudes that want you to turn down your shine
Insecure mindz
I sit back and smile
Yall fronting
Pretending to be other than what I see
Your words sound like trickery
Your touch feels like robbery
Your heart poisonous venom B
You believe in the lies then rise with the truth
That's no street cred you aint true
You poison the positive take away from the youth
You use laws and tactics to govern your rule
Over those who dare to go against being schooled
Pity a fool, your mortal mind
No reasoning no respect for the number 9

Try to break what don't need to be fixed

You and your minions try to dilute the real from its essence

Well I'm tired of being sick

I'm tired of false prophets

I'm tired of being uninspired

Tired of your lies

Tired of your games

Tired of your image

Tired of your ways

Solution I Will Be The Change

No Hate

If I hate you who would I be

I wouldn't begin to recognize me

I don't hate you, I have empathy

Courage assisted me in breaking free

Past illusions and intuned with reality

Life simplicity

Living on my terms, if you disagree brings no stress to me

Liberation celebrating, a liberated me

Free from the lies religion tells

Free from the mind control and indoctrinated spells

Free from the control of another's frequency

No made up language, no tones for you to channel

into me using my ancestral energy

You may be cunning yet ancestors bless me with the insight to see

His followers may be stuck yet I am free

I protect my soul; my spirits are hi

I sore through the skies

Unlimited and unbound

No fear, no regret, no guilt

Gratitude for what I found

No Hate Pt2

Conditioning is real

Only strong minds can break those chains mentally

Seeing past violation lines

No religion or culture, disguised as the explanation why

Weakness or wickedness

I can't judge or decide

All I know is you take instructions from a sick twisted mind

You believe and pacify lies

I was under his pretense once upon a time

I've lost all respect for those sheep

You won't get any of my time not even a peep

Culture vultures only in it for the shine

Couldn't make it in the real world, pretend time

We Live On The Air

Live out the pawns place on the chessboard of
someone's made up world in his mind
I resign from all positions away from your cult this time

Inner Peace

Needed space when too much thoughts are in my head
Too many opinions and outside influences can distort what we feel
They could never change the truth of what's real
Often criticize for my mind and how bright I shine
Am I to exist as I am
We all are divine
Its time to dwell in my peace of mind
Starting to discover who I am in this life
Who are friends when they find faults
What are memories precious thoughts
I was told all things take time
In a world filled with chaos
Peace is on my mind
Do I remember
Do I, do I remember?
Do I remember who I am
I couldn't remember
Now I know who I am, yes
I remember yes, I remember

www.ingramcontent.com/pod-product-compliance
Lightning Source LLC
Chambersburg PA
CBHW030559080526
44585CB00012B/429